BLACK HOLES

ENERGY

GALAXIES

GRAVITY

LIGHT

MYSTERIES OF
THE UNIVERSE

MASS & MATTER

SPACE & TIME

STARS

MYSTERIES OF
THE UNIVERSE

Stars

JIM WHITING

CREATIVE EDUCATION

Published by Creative Education
P.O. Box 227, Mankato, Minnesota 56002
Creative Education is an imprint of The Creative Company
www.thecreativecompany.us

Design and production by Blue Design
Art direction by Rita Marshall
Printed in the United States of America

Photographs by Getty Images (Steve Allen, Herbert Barraud, Margaret
Bourke-White/Time & Life Pictures, CBS Photo Archive, Ben Cooper,
Dmitri Kessel/Time Life Pictures, Joseph McNally, New York Times Co.,
Jay M. Pasachoff, SSPL), NASA (Hinode JAXA/NASA/PPARC, NASA,
NASA/Ames/JPL-Caltech, NASA/APL, NASA/CXC/JPL-Caltech/PSU/CfA,
NASA/ESA/Hubble/R. Sahai [JPL], NASA/ESA/Hubble Heritage Team,
NASA/JPL-Caltech/Kate Su [Steward Obs., U. Arizona] et al., NASA/JPL-
Caltech/UCLA, NASA/JPL-Caltech/UMD, NASA/Tod Strohmayer [GSFC]/
Dana Berry [Chandra X-Ray Observatory], NASA/STScl Digitized Sky
Survey/Noel Carboni)

Cover and folio illustration © 2011 Alex Ryan

Library of Congress Cataloging-in-Publication Data
Whiting, Jim.
Stars / by Jim Whiting.
p. cm. — (Mysteries of the universe)
Includes bibliographical references and index.
Summary: An examination of the science behind the astronomical
phenomena known as stars, including relevant theories and history-
making discoveries as well as topics of current and future research.
ISBN 978-1-60818-193-3
1. Stars—Juvenile literature. I. Title.

QB801.7.W455 2012
523.8—dc23   2011040148

First Edition
9 8 7 6 5 4 3 2 1

English astronomer Caroline Herschel

TABLE OF CONTENTS

The star-forming cloud Cepheus B, 2,400 light years from Earth

INTRODUCTION

For most of human history, the true nature of the universe was shrouded in myth and mystery. About 400 years ago, scientists began unraveling those mysteries. Their efforts were so successful that American **physicist** Albert Michelson wrote in 1894, "The more important fundamental laws and facts of physical science have all been discovered, and these are now so firmly established that the possibility of their ever being supplemented in consequence of new discoveries is exceedingly remote." William Thomson, Baron Kelvin, perhaps that era's most famous physicist, echoed Michelson: "There is nothing new to be discovered in physics now. All that remains is more and more precise measurement." Both men were wrong. Within a few years, scientists had revealed the makeup of the tiny **atom** and the unexpected vastness of outer space. Yet the universe doesn't yield its mysteries easily, and much remains to be discovered.

Few fields in science hold the same fascination for people as astronomy, the scientific study of stars. Stars have always been a source of wonder—and mystery.

Where did they come from? How long have they been there? How far away are they? And the questions keep coming. As we gaze upward on clear evenings, the twinkling of the stars doesn't give a hint of what's really going on. The heavens aren't as peaceful as they look. Then there's the ultimate mystery. Are we and all of Earth's creatures alone in the universe? Or are there planets containing life in some form circling those stars?

Baron Kelvin developed the absolute temperature scale

9

THE STARS AT NIGHT

There's a big mystery in the universe, and it has close to 100 "witnesses" that might provide some answers. A few are human figures: a king, a queen, a captive, a hunter, a hero, a herdsman. Others are representatives of the animal kingdom, with creatures ranging from a bull, a bear, and birds to a fox, fowl, and fish.

These universal witnesses are actually constellations, or groups of stars that are thought to resemble certain people, animals, or even objects. The International Astronomical Union officially recognizes 88 constellations today. Some date back thousands of years to **Babylonian** times, while others—such as Microscopium and Telescopium, honoring their namesake instruments and dating to the 18th century—are fairly recent. In total, the "Great 88" represent a hefty percentage of the stars we can see with the naked eye.

The mystery of the stars goes back nearly 14 billion years to the very origins of the universe. While they can't tell us what happened at the beginning, the stars of the 88 constellations have been around long enough—in most cases between 1 and 10 billion years—to see some pretty amazing things. In recent years, we've had the chance to see some of those things ourselves as **stellar** mysteries start to reveal themselves.

The people who study these mysteries are known as astronomers. The roots of the word "astronomy" suggest the importance of the constellations in understanding the heavens. It comes from two Greek words, *astron*, or "star," and *nomos*, or "arranging." So astronomers are literally "people who arrange the stars."

Astronomy isn't the same as astrology, though the origins of the two fields are closely linked, and their names were virtually interchangeable until about the 1400s. Astrology grew out of the ancient belief that stars and planets directly influence people's lives. The first astrologers sought practical uses for astronomy, applying patterns of heavenly phenomena to events on Earth and measuring time. By the 1700s, astrology was defined

ORION

Gemini.

Via

Lactea

Monoceros.

Æquator.

Canis Major

Lepus

The Witch Head Nebula reflects
blue light from its star, Rigel

as "reading influences of the stars and their effects on human destiny." Meanwhile, astronomy claimed the more rational, scientific side of observing the heavens.

To astronomers, the 2,500 or so stars we can see with the naked eye—along with the billions more visible with telescopes—are unique. By analyzing the light of each star, astronomers can determine its exact brightness, color, and temperature. They know what composes stars and how fast they move through the heavens. They can even predict where stars will be many centuries from now.

Astronomers divide stars into seven classes based on their surface temperatures (which in turn are related to their primary coloration). Red stars have the lowest temperatures, under 3,500 kelvin (5,840 °F). At the opposite extreme are blue stars, with temperatures from 10,000 to upwards of 50,000 kelvin (17,540 to 89,540 °F). Our sun is about a third of the way up the scale, in a group of stars with temperatures ranging from 5,000 to 6,000 kelvin (8,540 to 10,340 °F).

The smallest and most numerous stars in the universe are red dwarfs. They range in size from a few times smaller than our sun to a hundred times smaller. They are red because their temperature is comparatively low. Because they are so small and so faint, they will burn for tens of billions of years.

Our sun is a yellow star. Yellow stars are larger than red dwarfs and burn their hydrogen fuel more rapidly. Even so, they can last for a long time. Astronomers believe that the sun is about halfway through a 10-billion-year life cycle. Other yellow stars follow similar time frames.

The largest stars are blue giants, which can generate 10,000 times the amount of energy of our sun or more. The blue supergiant star Rigel, one of the "feet" in the constellation of Orion, is 25 times larger than the sun. Because these stars are so

White dwarfs orbiting each other

massive and burn so much fuel, they last for only hundreds of millions of years.

Stars big and small are grouped together into galaxies. These are systems of stars held together by mutual **gravitational** attraction and separated from similar systems by vast regions of space. The most well-known galaxy is our own Milky Way, which, according to some astronomers, contains 400 billion stars. In turn, the Milky Way is just 1 of an estimated 100 billion galaxies in the universe.

It seems as if the stars in the skies are unchanging. But astronomers have shown us that, just like people, stars are born, live for a long time, and then die. Unlike people, stars' lifetimes are often reckoned in billions of years. They form out of clouds of stellar dust and other bits of matter—including fragments of dead stars. This process often takes millions of years to complete.

In essence, stars are giant balls of burning gases, primarily hydrogen and helium. The outward push of the energy created by such burning balances the inward pressure of the force of gravity. Eventually, the supply of gas begins to run out. There is no longer enough outward pressure. What happens at that point largely depends on the star's original size.

Stars similar in size to our sun tend to lose their outer layers of gases and dust over time. These castoffs, known as **planetary nebulae**, drift off into space, leaving behind a small star called a white dwarf. Its remaining material is very tightly packed, and a normal-sized person on a white dwarf would weigh millions of pounds because of the star's enormous gravity. White dwarfs have no more nuclear fuel to burn, so they gradually cool.

Sometimes a star larger than the sun becomes part of a spectacular event called a supernova, which occurs when the star explodes near the end of its lifetime. It becomes up to a million times brighter than normal. The violence of the explosion combines **protons** and **electrons** to form **neutrons**, which join with other neutrons to form a mass far more dense than a white dwarf. This is called a neutron star.

In still larger stars, gravitational forces crush the matter even further, to the size of

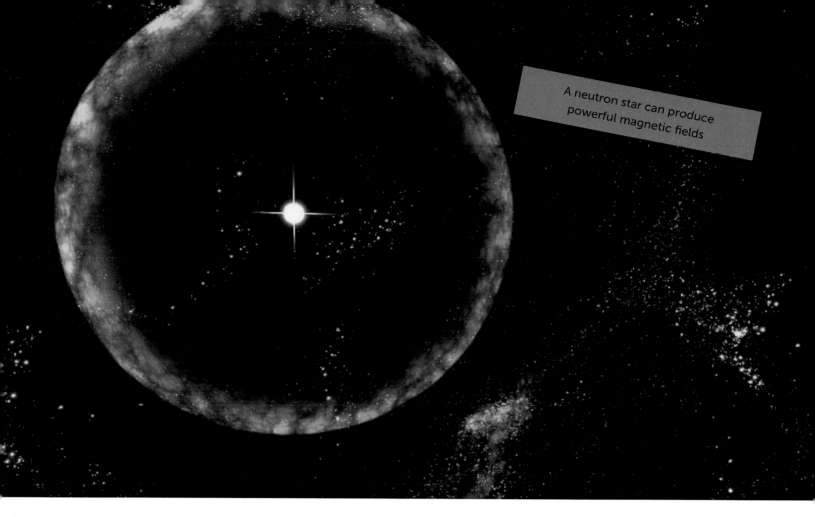

A neutron star can produce powerful magnetic fields

a pinhead. The gravitational pull of such a collapsed star is so strong that not even light can escape. This is a black hole. Because they emit no light, black holes can't be observed directly. Often, they are close to another star and pull gas from the surface of this other star. Heat from the gas is sometimes emitted as **X-rays**, which can be detected.

Stars are unbelievably far away. The numbers get so high that astronomers devised a measurement called a light year, the distance that light travels in a year, to keep from getting bogged down in numbers containing long strings of zeroes. A light year represents about 6 trillion miles (9.5 trillion km) and is obtained by multiplying the speed of light per second (186,282 miles, or 299,792 km) by the number of seconds in a year (31,557,600).

The closest star to Earth is the sun. It's a mere 93 million miles (150 million km) away! The next closest star is Proxima Centauri, about 4.2 light years away. That's a distance of about 24 trillion miles (40 trillion km). Time and distance become mind-boggling in their enormity where stars are concerned. For example, an explosion that ripped a star apart might have happened millions of years ago, but we're just seeing it now. We have no idea what is going on in the star's present, and we won't know for millions of years!

Away from cities, the night sky
can be seen clearly

STARGAZING—THEN AND NOW

From the dawn of civilization, humans have studied the sky. Month after month, year after year, century after century, early astronomers made painstaking measurements of the movements of the sun, the moon, and the stars. They found that these heavenly bodies followed regular paths. This regularity, especially of the sun and moon, led to the development of calendars. Calendars were vital to societies that depended on crops for food and **commerce** because they helped farmers know when to start planting their crops. Such knowledge had a special value in Egypt, where the land was almost entirely barren desert. Once a year, though, the Nile River overflowed its banks, depositing nutrients for several miles inland and making it possible to grow crops. Thousands of years ago, the Egyptians realized that Sirius—the brightest star in the sky—began rising at dawn just before this overflow. They built their calendar around this phenomenon.

Another important star to the ancients was Polaris, the North Star. It showed which direction was north. This knowledge was especially valuable to sailors, who used it to help navigate across the often featureless seas, and to American slaves trying to escape northward in the 19th century. Since they could travel more secretly at night, to them, the North Star pointed the way to freedom.

Many years of observations led ancient astronomers to the realization that five stars acted differently from the hundreds of others they could see. These five followed seemingly random routes, sometimes appearing to speed up, slow down, or even go backwards. Named for their "wandering" ways, they eventually became known as planets: Mercury, Venus, Mars, Jupiter, and Saturn. Along with the sun and moon, the planets were regarded as so important that they were given godlike powers and worshiped. In many civilizations—including ours—the seven days of the week were named after the celestial bodies (and other gods).

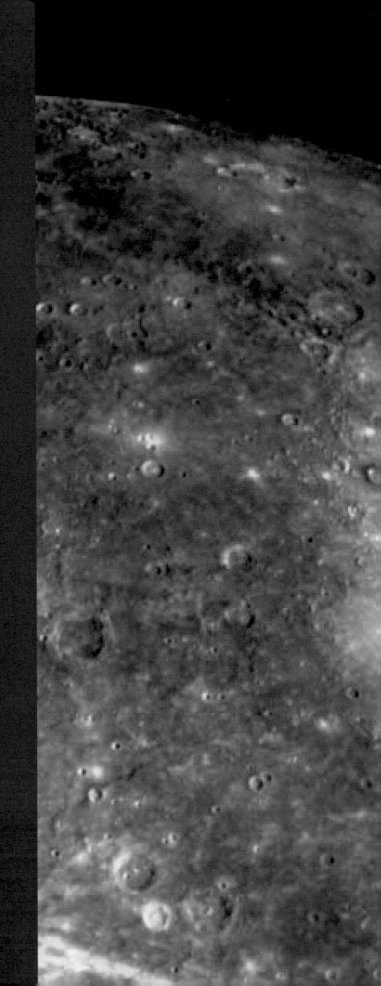

By the time of the Greek thinker Aristotle, astronomers had developed a way of organizing the universe that was modeled on Earth being at the center of several revolving and concentric spheres. The moon was in the first sphere, Mercury was in the second, and Venus was in the third. The sun, Mars, Jupiter, and Saturn were in the next four. All the stars were in the eighth sphere, the farthest from Earth. This geocentric universe worked well for the Greeks, who believed that Earth was changeable and subject to decay. The heavens, on the other hand, were perfect and unchanging.

Around 129 B.C., a Greek named Hipparchus invented a ranking system for the brightness of stars. The brightest ones he rated at the first magnitude, while the lowest class of barely visible stars occupied the sixth magnitude. The rest fell in between. This basic idea remains in use today.

Mercury has a thick iron core
and is the closest planet to the sun

The comet Hartley 2

Scientists have long sought an explanation for the beginning of the universe. Many now believe that it began about 13.7 billion years ago in an explosive event called the Big Bang. According to this theory, time, space, and matter did not exist prior to the Big Bang. In the first fraction of a second after the explosion, energy was turned into a few pounds of matter. In that instant, the universe was almost incredibly hot and very dense. In another fraction of a second, the universe expanded many billions of times, starting to cool as time began. Eventually this expansion generated the four fundamental forces that control the universe: gravity, the force that keeps stars and planets in **orbit**; the strong nuclear force, which keeps the nuclei of atoms together; the weak nuclear force, which regulates radiation and therefore allows the stars to shine; and electromagnetism, which governs the behavior of electricity and magnetism. For millions and millions of years, the universe was dark. Then clouds of matter began to coalesce and fuse, and finally, over many more millions of years, that matter became stars.

As the years went by, it became increasingly difficult to account for the erratic movements of the planets and make them fit into circles, though. Finally, in the second century A.D., the Greek astronomer Claudius Ptolemy devised a complicated system of epicycles, or circles-within-circles. His book the *Almagest* (*The Great Compilation*) became the standard astronomy reference text for nearly 1,500 years as the theory of a geocentric universe went virtually unchallenged in the Western world, particularly in the countries of southern and western Europe.

Starting with Polish astronomer Nicolaus Copernicus, astronomers began chipping away at the geocentric view. One big step came in 1572. Danish astronomer Tycho Brahe observed what appeared to be a bright new star in the constellation Cassiopeia. He also studied **comets** extensively. To Aristotle and the Greeks, comets had simply been phenomena located within Earth's atmosphere. Brahe demonstrated that comets traveled far beyond Earth and showed that the heavens were subject

Stars continue to form in the
Large Magellanic Cloud

to change. Apart from his identification of what is known as Halley's Comet, English astronomer Edmund Halley also noted that the positions of certain "fixed stars" had changed since the days of Hipparchus and Ptolemy.

By that time, belief in the geocentric universe was on the wane. When the telescope was invented in 1609, humans gained the ability to probe the skies far more deeply and discover millions of previously unknown stars. This resulted in an alteration to Hipparchus's magnitude ranking system. As increasingly fainter stars were revealed, the scale had to be adjusted accordingly, eventually reaching the 31st magnitude.

There were changes at the other end of the scale as well. Some first-magnitude stars were found to be brighter than others. Four of them—Rigel, Capella, Arcturus, and Vega—were reclassified as magnitude 0, and Sirius—the brightest of all—became magnitude -1.44. Other celestial bodies went even farther down the scale: Venus was -4.4, the full moon -12.5, and the sun -26.7.

Adjustments in the magnitude scale were made possible, in part, by the data available in the cataloging systems available at that time. The Royal Observatory at Greenwich, England, was established in 1676 to provide a star catalog to help British sailors navigate around the globe. At about the same time, a series of observers began to provide increasingly accurate measurements of the speed of light as well. In the mid-18th century, French astronomer Charles Messier began observing **nebulae** in deep space and compiling a list of them in the Messier catalog, which would eventually include more than 100 entries and prove invaluable to the work of future astronomers.

Yet as the 20th century dawned, people still had no idea how vast the universe actually was. Until then, astronomers believed that the universe consisted of one galaxy: our own Milky Way. That belief was shattered almost overnight in the 1920s. It soon became apparent that the number of stars and galaxies was far greater than anyone had ever anticipated. On top of that, the universe was expanding—and it was expanding in all directions, not just away from our solar system.

Most astronomical research came to a halt with the outbreak of World War II in 1939. Then the Cold War and resulting arms race between the Soviet Union and the United States absorbed much of the world's scientific energy until the 1960s, when people turned their attention to outer space again, this time with the intention of exploring it with spacecraft and occupying it with satellites.

When astronomers resumed their sweeps of the skies, they were aided by new methods of probing the heavens, such as X-ray telescopes, radio telescopes, and

New Mexico's Very Large Array has 27 radio antennas

Actor Orson Welles doing a radio broadcast in 1938

Martian Invasion

Published in 1898, British author H. G. Wells's *War of the Worlds* was among the first novels to deal with life from other planets. As the title suggests, the encounter wasn't peaceful. According to Wells, "across the gulf of space, minds that are to our minds as ours are to those of the beasts that perish, intellects vast and cool and unsympathetic, regarded this earth with envious eyes, and slowly and surely drew their plans against us." These "minds" were on Mars. Using superior weapons, they easily overcame the earthlings' resistance. But they were destroyed by bacterial infections. The book was popular and inspired many spin-offs, including a famous radio broadcast on Halloween Eve in 1938. At the start of that show, actor and director Orson Welles said that the production was a work of the imagination. However, many listeners missed that announcement. The on-the-spot newscast style sounded like a real invasion and caused thousands of people to panic. As a boy, American scientist Robert Goddard read *War of the Worlds* and was inspired to devote his life to rocket research. He became an important pioneer in the field that eventually developed powerful rockets that sent instruments into Earth orbit to study the stars.

infrared telescopes, which allowed astronomers to see different wavelengths of light and to detect celestial bodies at great distances. Eventually telescopes were launched into Earth orbit, where the lack of atmospheric interference vastly improved their ability to gather information. Now astronomers gazed on a very different universe from the apparently orderly, almost mystical procession that people had observed for several millennia. As American astronomer Kimberly Weaver says, "Our universe is explosive and violent. The ominous black holes, **plasma jets**, stellar explosions, and cosmic collisions ... are real galactic events." It was time to discover what stars truly had in store.

Perhaps the greatest mystery involving stars is whether they have planets capable of supporting life. From a statistical point of view, with the trillions and trillions of stars in the universe, the possibility seems likely. Astronomers have made great strides in the past few years in finding possible new worlds. If we do find that we are not alone, it would probably be the most momentous event in the history of the universe.

Astronomer William Herschel, 1814

STARS

28

STELLAR RESEARCHERS

Italian physicist and astronomer Galileo Galilei (1564–1642) is one of the key figures in stellar research. While he didn't build the first telescope, he did make one in 1609 that was good enough to begin probing the heavens. He was the first person to see stars invisible to the naked eye and add to Hipparchus's magnitude system. As Galileo wrote in his 1610 book *Sidereus Nuncius* (*Starry Messenger*), "With the glass you will detect below stars of the sixth magnitude such a crowd of others that escape natural sight that it is hardly believable. The largest of these … we may designate as of the seventh magnitude."

English physicist Isaac Newton (1643–1727) improved on Galileo's design by using mirrors instead of lenses in his **reflecting telescope**. Newton was able to determine that the same force—gravity—that kept things on Earth from drifting off into space permeated the entire universe. He also showed that visible light was a **spectrum** of seven different colors—red, orange, yellow, blue, green, indigo, and violet.

German-born British astronomer William Herschel (1738–1822) built on Newton's work by separating the **constituent** colors of the visible light spectrum and taking their temperatures. Noticing that there was more energy beyond the red end of the scale, Herschel discovered infrared light in 1800. That laid the foundation for **spectroscopy**, one of the most important branches of science that modern astronomers use to learn how stars change over time.

William's sister Caroline Herschel (1750–1848) discovered eight comets and compiled a catalog of thousands of stellar phenomena. John Herschel (1792–1871), William's son, catalogued many stars in the Southern Hemisphere and named the then known moons of Saturn and Uranus. Modern English astronomers Heather Couper and Nigel Henbest credit the Herschels as being among the most important figures in the history of astronomy, saying that the family of scientists "opened up the heavens—clearing the path for astronomers to address the architecture of our Solar System."

At the end of the 19th century, American astronomer George Ellery Hale (1868–1938) invented the spectroheliograph, an instrument that creates a photographic image of the sun at one wavelength of light to render details of its surface. Later in his career he discovered that sunspots had **magnetic fields** and was able to measure the strength of those fields. These accomplishments helped identify the chemical and physical properties of stars. However, Hale's greatest contribution to astronomy was founding and overseeing some of the most important observatories in the U.S. He began in 1897 with the Yerkes Observatory in Wisconsin. It houses the world's largest **refracting telescope**, with a lens measuring 40 inches (102 cm) in diameter.

Thanks to recent advancements in grinding mirrors to achieve exact dimensions, Hale soon realized that the future of astronomy lay with reflecting telescopes and their superior ability to gather light from space. He moved to California, where the viewing conditions were better, and built the Mt. Wilson Observatory near Los Angeles. His first instrument was a 60-inch (152 cm) reflecting telescope in 1908—at the time, the world's largest telescope. Nine years later came the 100-inch (254 cm) Hooker Telescope, also at Mt. Wilson. Hale capped his career with the Palomar Observatory between Los Angeles and San Diego, which opened in 1948 with the 200-inch (508 cm) Hale Telescope. It was a remarkable technical accomplishment, as most telescopes with mirrors that large tended to sag under their own weight.

American astronomer Edwin Hubble (1889–1953) was one of the main beneficiaries of Hale's work. Using the Hooker Telescope, he studied M31 (object number 31 in Messier's catalog). What had looked hazy to Messier now appeared in sharp focus as a huge collection of stars, and Hubble's calculations placed it at a distance of more than one million miles (1.6 million km) away, far beyond the borders of the Milky Way.

Looking down on the Hooker Telescope at the Mt. Wilson Observatory

In short, it was another galaxy, whose existence had been totally unexpected. It quickly became apparent that there were many more galaxies, the number of which would eventually extend into the billions.

In 1929, Hubble used what is known as the Doppler Effect to prove that the universe was expanding. The effect is like an ambulance siren. As an ambulance gets closer, the sound of its siren is pitched at a higher level because the wavelengths are bunched up. As it moves away, the wavelengths get longer, and the noise becomes increasingly faint. The same thing happens with light waves from stars. As the waves recede, they move toward the longer end of the spectrum, which is red. This is known as the red shift. The faster the stars are moving, the greater the red shift becomes. Because the farthest galaxies Hubble observed were the reddest, this meant that they were moving away from Earth—and from each other. The situation

Astronomer Edwin Hubble, circa 1945

was somewhat similar to what happens when you paint dots on a gigantic balloon and then inflate it. The larger it gets, the farther away the dots become from the center and from each other.

As Hubble was revolutionizing our concepts of the size and composition of the universe, English-American astronomy student Cecilia Payne-Gaposchkin (1900–79) wrote what one **astrophysicist** said was the most brilliant **doctoral dissertation** in the history of astronomy. Payne-Gaposchkin was the first to show that the sun is composed almost entirely of the elements hydrogen and helium; in fact, she found that hydrogen makes up more than three-quarters of the sun's total mass and is a million times more prevalent than any other element. Since all stars operate on principles similar to what people were able to observe in the sun, this discovery implied that hydrogen was by far the most common element in the universe.

Although Payne-Gaposchkin's conclusion was initially rejected because it was so different from the prevailing view—not long before that, many people had thought the sun burned coal—it became obvious that she was correct within a few years. Her discovery paved the way for German-American physicist Hans Bethe (1906–2005) to explain how stars produce light and energy. Stars, in a sense, are great furnaces fueled by hydrogen atoms. Bethe studied how hydrogen atoms reacted in laboratories on Earth and calculated what would happen to them under the vastly increased temperatures and pressure of stars during a process called fusion.

In the turbulent and unbelievably hot (25,000,000 °F, or 14,000,000 °C) stellar core, the protons of hydrogen atoms continuously collide with each other. Frequently, these collisions are powerful enough to overcome the natural electromagnetic repulsion of positively charged particles, and the protons of two hydrogen atoms fuse, or join. Two of these fused nuclei in turn fuse with each other, forming the nucleus of a helium atom. During this process, a minute amount of matter is lost. According to German-born physicist Albert Einstein's famous **equation** $E=mc^2$ (energy equals mass times the speed of light squared, or multiplied by itself), even a tiny bit of mass generates massive amounts of energy.

Buffeted by countless numbers of collisions, this energy slowly makes its way from the center of a star to the surface. For the sun, with its diameter of approximately 870,000 miles (1,400,129 km), estimates of the time this journey takes range from a few thousand years to upwards of a million years. Eight minutes after it reaches the sun's surface, energy in the form of light arrives on Earth.

STELLAR RESEARCHERS

This composite image of the solar system was made from a combination of pictures

ANYBODY OUT THERE?

For most people, the key mystery regarding stars is whether planets capable of supporting life orbit around them. For centuries, people throughout the world have seen what they believe are unidentified flying objects, or UFOs. While many, if not most, of these sightings can be explained in terms of known quantities, a few cannot. Some people think these unexplainable sightings are spacecraft from beyond Earth.

Whether so-called ufologists are correct, astronomers continue to search the heavens for exoplanets, or planets that orbit stars outside the solar system. The search is challenging. Exoplanets are almost invisible, even to the most powerful optical telescopes. The light they emit is only a fraction of what their parent star gives off, and glare from that star's light makes even that minute amount virtually undetectable. Only a handful of exoplanets (believed to be considerably larger than Jupiter and at a significant distance from their parent star) are dimly visible from Earth.

Astronomers rely on a variety of indirect methods to determine an exoplanet's existence, size, and distance from its star. In his general theory of relativity, presented in 1915, Albert Einstein proved that stars bend light due to their gravitational pull. Exoplanets do this, too. So if light from a distant star passes an exoplanet, it bends slightly. Astronomers measure this tiny change, which suggests the existence of an exoplanet. Next, because an exoplanet has a small gravitational pull on its star, causing a slight "wobble," measuring the amount of wobble provides clues of the planet's size. When an exoplanet passes in front of its star, the star's light dims slightly. An astronomer is often able to gauge the exoplanet's relative size by observing how bright or dim the light from the star is. This method also provides some clues as to the exoplanet's size; the larger it is, the more the light changes.

The first confirmed identification of an exoplanet orbiting a star came in 1995, with the star 51 Pegasi in the constellation Pegasus, which is just under 51 light years away. By

2000, astronomers had found 30 more.
They identified another 148 exoplanets
between 2000 and 2005 and more than
doubled that tally in the following 5 years.
Improved devices, such as telescopes
in Earth orbit, not only identify more
exoplanets but also make it possible to
discover smaller ones, which are more
likely to sustain life.

In 2008, the National Aeronautics and
Space Administration (NASA)'s Spitzer
Space Telescope made such a discovery.
The observatory satellite detected a
dust cloud surrounding a star about
430 light years away. "What we think
we're seeing is the actual formation of a
planet—terrestrial planet—a rocky planet
like the Earth, around the star," said Dr.
Carey Lisse, a senior research scientist at
Johns Hopkins Applied Physics Laboratory
in Laurel, Maryland. Lisse and his fellow
scientists believed the relatively young
star was just the right age—10 to 16 million
years old—for planet formation, but it
was difficult to know for sure. Earth took
millions of years just to form, and it has

The Kepler-10 star system: exoplanets Kepler-10b (dark spot against sun) and Kepler-10c (at left)

The astronauts in *2001* make a plan to deactivate HAL

Way beyond the Moon

Released in 1968, the movie *2001: A Space Odyssey* provided an early glimpse of what interstellar travel might involve. It foresaw a future in which trips to the moon—where a human colony had been established—were commonplace, and a deep-space vehicle was prepared to voyage into the unknown cosmos. The film begins with a battle between two groups of early humans in the shadow of a strange black **monolith**. One kills a member of the rival group with a dead animal's thigh bone, then happily hurls the bone into the air. It turns into a space station, symbolizing the ability of humans to overcome gravity and venture into space. The film continues with a long voyage to Jupiter in search of the monolith's origins. During this voyage, the "villain"—a computer named HAL—tries to sabotage the mission. In an ending that many people find confusing, the surviving astronaut appears to find another monolith and becomes transformed. The film depicts the challenges that stellar astronauts might encounter during such a voyage, as some crew members are kept in a state of suspended animation, while those needed to operate the spacecraft exercise regularly and are allowed to converse briefly with their loved ones back on Earth.

taken billions of years to evolve to its present state.

Just finding an exoplanet isn't enough to determine whether it contains life. Its position relative to the star it orbits is crucial. If it's too close, the heat will fry everything, as is the case in our own solar system with Mercury. Temperatures there can exceed 700 °F (371 °C). If the planet is too far away, as is the case on Neptune, where the temperature can dip below -350 °F (-212 °C), any water would be perpetually frozen and thereby make life as we know it impossible to sustain. Astronomers seek exoplanets they describe as "Goldilocks planets"—those in just the right position to support life by containing liquid water and an atmosphere.

Accordingly, there was great excitement late in 2010 when astronomers at Hawaii's W. M. Keck Observatory announced they had found an exoplanet that could fit that Goldilocks description, using data obtained over an 11-year period. The planet was among 6 orbiting a star named Gliese 581, just 20 light years away. Doubts quickly emerged, though. Early in 2011, astrostatistics expert Philip Gregory of the University of British Columbia analyzed the same data and said, "I don't find anything.... For the time

41

being, the world does not have data that's good enough to claim the planet."

Such data could be forthcoming in the near future. Early in 2009, NASA launched the Kepler Space Telescope into orbit around the sun on a mission that could last for up to six years, providing ample time to eliminate "false positives," or sightings that at first appear to be valid but are later ruled out for some reason. The key element in Kepler's design is a super-sensitive camera, the largest ever sent into space. The telescope soon discovered its first Earth-sized planetary candidates, including some in the habitable zone, where water appears to be available. Further research is necessary to determine whether the "candidates" could be planets, but as William Borucki, the Kepler mission's principal investigator, noted, "The fact that we've found so many planet candidates in such a tiny fraction of the sky [Kepler's field of view covers just 1/400th of the sky] suggests there are countless planets orbiting sun-like stars in our galaxy." "We went from 0 to 68 Earth-sized planet candidates and 0 to 54 candidates in the habitable zone," he continued, "some of which could have moons with liquid water."

No doubt the coming years will continue to bring exciting discoveries as astronomers continue to search the far reaches of the universe for signs of life. And stars themselves still hold plenty of mysteries. Chief among them is how many stars there are in the universe. Based on the number of stars in the Milky Way, astronomers now estimate that there could be as many as 300 sextillion (a trillion multiplied by 300 billion, or 3 followed by 23 zeroes—300,000,000,000,000,000,000,000) stars.

Based on recent studies of eight **elliptical galaxies**, Yale University astronomer Pieter van Dokkum and Harvard astrophysicist Charlie Conroy of the Keck Observatory believe that this staggering number might be closer to actuality than the previous figure of 100 sextillion. Elliptical galaxies compose about a third of the 100 billion to 1 trillion galaxies in the universe. Each elliptical galaxy may have many more red dwarf stars than originally believed—as much as 10 to 20 times more—upping their total to between

The Spitzer Space Telescope detected infrared radiation from the Helix Nebula

High up in Hawaii

Nearly everyone associates Hawaii with warm sun, sandy beaches, and bathing suits. But there's one place on the Big Island that sees seasonal snow and people wearing heavy coats. It's the Observatories at Mauna Kea, perched at an altitude of nearly 13,780 feet (4,200 m). The site boasts 13 telescopes—administered by several nations—that take advantage of Mauna Kea's special conditions, with its dark nighttime skies, minimal atmospheric interference, and very little water vapor. Perhaps the most significant installation is the W. M. Keck Observatory. Its twin telescopes feature mirrors 33 feet (10 m) in diameter, making them the world's second-largest optical telescopes. The mirrors in turn consist of 36 hexagonal, or 6-sided, segments, which are computer-adjusted twice every second to counteract the effects of gravity as the telescope tracks objects across the sky. Several highly sophisticated instruments have allowed the Keck Observatory to perform various and significant studies of the universe during the short time it's been open. The first telescope became operational in 1993, followed by the second three years later. The Keck Observatory announced its discovery of the first "Goldilocks planet" in 2010. According to Mario R. Perez, Keck program scientist, "Keck is once again proving itself an amazing tool for scientific research."

1 and 10 trillion, rather than 100 billion. When it comes to red dwarfs and elliptical galaxies, though, van Dokkum cautioned that astronomers "have made the mistake of assuming that the Milky Way was typical of all galaxies in the universe." Accordingly, "we shouldn't make the mistake of assuming that these eight elliptical galaxies are representatives for all elliptical galaxies in the universe," he said.

Van Dokkum makes a good point. Less than a century ago, astronomers thought the Milky Way was the extent of the universe. The rapid increase in improved techniques and tools since then has resulted in better knowledge about the stars. Yet there is still much to be learned, and what we believe to be true today may be disproved by future discoveries. One thing, however, remains unchanged. On a clear night, we gaze upward with the same wonder as our ancestors did thousands of years ago. And we continue to reach for the stars.

The Keck domes are air-conditioned to keep temperatures at or below freezing

ENDNOTES

astrophysicist — a person who studies the branch of astronomy that deals with the physical nature of the universe

atom — the smallest part of an element with the chemical properties of that element

Babylonian — of or relating to Babylon, a city-state in present-day Iraq that originated more than 4,000 years ago; for a time, Babylon was probably the world's largest city

comets — celestial objects in the solar system that orbit the sun and consist of small frozen heads composed of several frozen gases and water, plus long, vaporous tails

commerce — the buying and selling of products

constituent — serving as one part of a larger entity

doctoral dissertation — a lengthy research paper written as part of the requirement to receive a PhD (doctor of philosophy), the highest degree awarded by colleges and universities

electrons — tiny, negatively charged particles that orbit the nucleus, or center, of atoms

elliptical galaxies — galaxies with oval shapes and no apparent internal structure or spiral arms

equation — a mathematical statement showing the equivalence of two quantities by linking them with an equals sign (=)

geocentric — relating to the ancient belief that Earth is the center of the universe

gravitational — having to do with gravity, the force of attraction between all masses in the universe that causes objects to fall toward the center of the earth, and which keeps the moon in steady orbit around Earth and the planets in orbit around the sun

infrared — a type of light that cannot be seen by humans; its wavelength is longer than visible light's

magnetic fields — lines of force that surround a magnet or charged particle and include two magnetic poles

magnitude — the degree of brightness of a star or the class of a star as determined by its brightness

monolith — a single large stone

nebulae — bright clouds of dust and gases in space, and the former term for galaxies; a single such cloud is a nebula

neutrons — tiny, uncharged particles found in the nucleus, or center, of an atom

orbit — the curved path that a celestial object takes around a larger celestial object

physicist — a person who studies matter and motion through space and time in an effort to discover the physical laws of the universe

planetary nebulae — expanding and glowing clouds of gas released by a star during the final stages of its existence

plasma jets — bursts of X-rays and other materials ejected high into space from dying stars

protons — tiny, positively charged particles found in the nucleus, or center, of an atom

reflecting telescope — a telescope that uses one or more curved mirrors to reflect light and form an image that is enlarged by an eyepiece

refracting telescope — the earliest form of an optical telescope; it uses lenses to form and magnify an image based on the refraction, or bending, of light

spectroscopy — the branch of science concerned with analyzing light and matter by dividing light into its seven colors

spectrum — a band of colors or the entire range of wavelengths of electromagnetic radiation

stellar — of or relating to stars

X-rays — forms of electromagnetic radiation with shorter wavelengths than visible light and capable of penetrating solids

WEB SITES

Ask an Astrophysicist: The Physics of Stars
http://imagine.gsfc.nasa.gov/docs/ask_astro/stars.html
Get all your star questions answered here, and find new resources for further research.

International Astronomical Union: The Constellations
http://www.iau.org/public/constellations/
Learn how to pronounce the names of constellations and see the charts that depict their shapes.

SELECTED BIBLIOGRAPHY

Asimov, Isaac. *Isaac Asimov's Guide to Earth and Space*. New York: Random House, 1991.

Baker, Joanne. *50 Physics Ideas You Really Need to Know*. London: Quercus Publishing, 2007.

Couper, Heather, and Nigel Henbest. *The History of Astronomy*. Buffalo, N.Y.: Firefly Books, 2007.

Krumenaker, Larry, ed. *The Characteristics and the Life Cycle of Stars: An Anthology of Current Thought*. New York: Rosen, 2006.

Levy, David H., and Wendee Wallach-Levy. *Cosmic Discoveries: The Wonders of Astronomy*. Amherst, N.Y.: Prometheus Books, 2001.

Nicolson, Iain. *Stars and Supernovas*. New York: DK Publishing, 2001.

Tyson, Neil deGrasse. *Death by Black Hole: And Other Cosmic Quandaries*. New York: W. W. Norton, 2007.

Weaver, Kimberly. *The Violent Universe: Joyrides through the X-ray Cosmos*. Baltimore: Johns Hopkins University Press, 2005.

47

INDEX